Isaiah Strong

Written by:
Isaiah Melendez

Isaiah Strong

Copyright © 2019 by Isaiah Melendez. All rights reserved.

No rights claimed for public domain material, all rights reserved.
No parts of this publication may be reproduced, stored in any retrieval system,
or transmitted in any form or by any means, electronic, mechanical, recording,
or otherwise, without the prior written permission of the author.
Violations may be subject to civil or criminal penalties.

ISBN:
978-1-63308-503-9 (paperback)
978-1-63308-504-6 (ebook)

Interior and Cover Design by *R'tor John D. Maghuyop*

CHALFANT ECKERT
PUBLISHING

1028 S Bishop Avenue, Dept. 178
Rolla, MO 65401

Printed in United States of America

Isaiah Strong

Written by:
Isaiah Melendez

Thank you

I would like to thank all those who emotionally supported me since day one, friends and family. My dad, Joseph, older brother, Xavier Reyes, and sister, Jadalynn Reyes. My grandparents, Carmen and Pedro Perez, my Uncle Pedro, and aunts, Raysa and Vivian. David Medina and family.

Neumors Specialty care staff and Wolfson Hospital, best doctors and Nurses ever. Kristen Saunders, social worker.

Latin American Motorcycle Association worldwide, especially Tanya Alcantara.

US Legal Services.

All the cancer foundations that assisted with gifts, toys, prayers and financial assistance, especially Jay Fund, V for Victory, Dreams Come True, Leukemia and Lymphoma Society.

To all our friends from New York, Colorado, and Florida. Tina Richardson and family, Caridad Tillman and family. To my 2 uncles, Lulu and Ricky Perez. May they rest in peace.

And of course, my mom. My rock since day one.

Meet Isaiah

A brave boy, just five years old

He may be young

But he has a story to be told

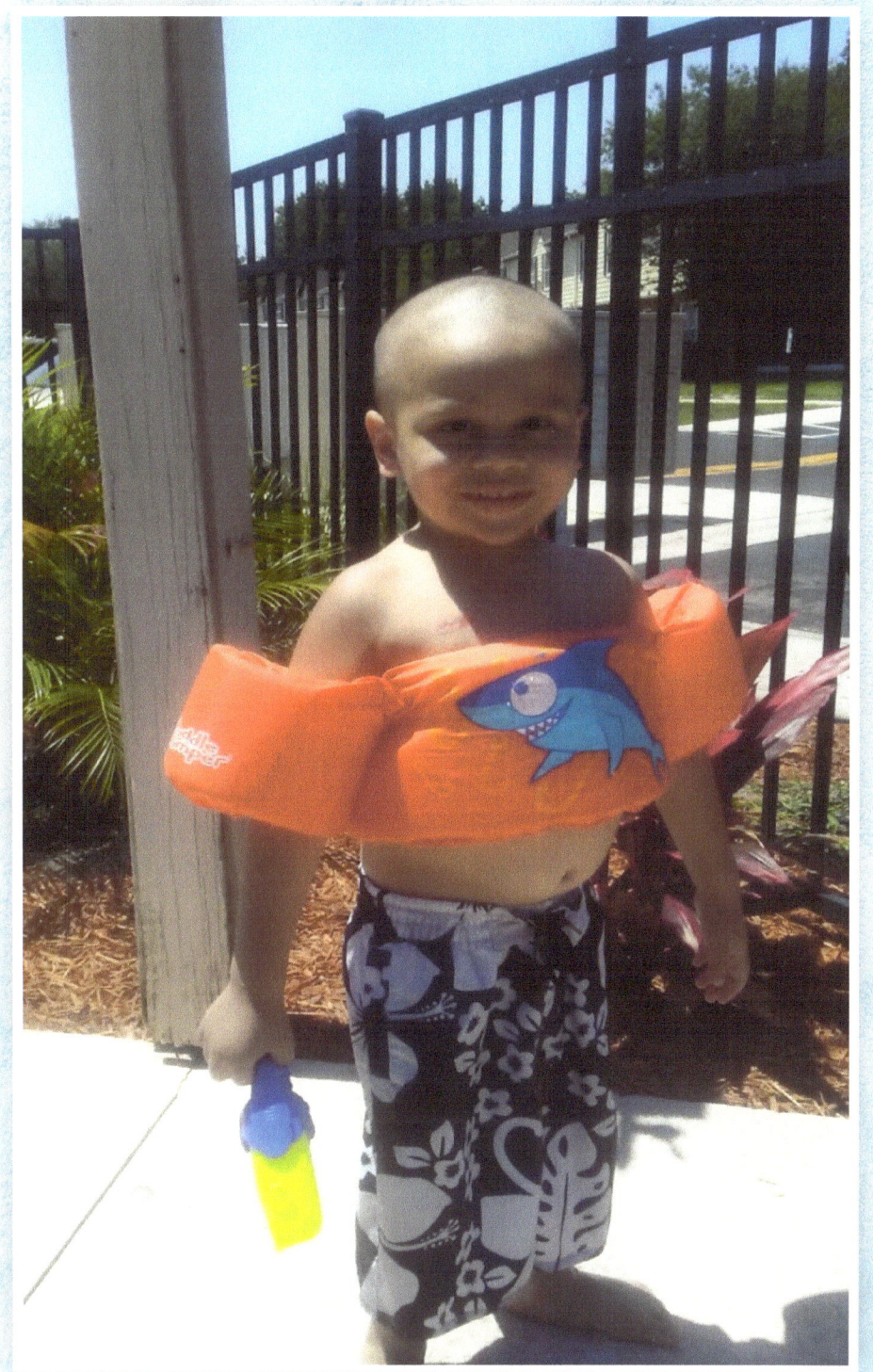

Isaiah may look like a normal kid

He plays all day long

But Isaiah is a true warrior

Courageous and strong

His story could turn anyone

Into a believer

Isaiah and family's lives

All changed with a fever

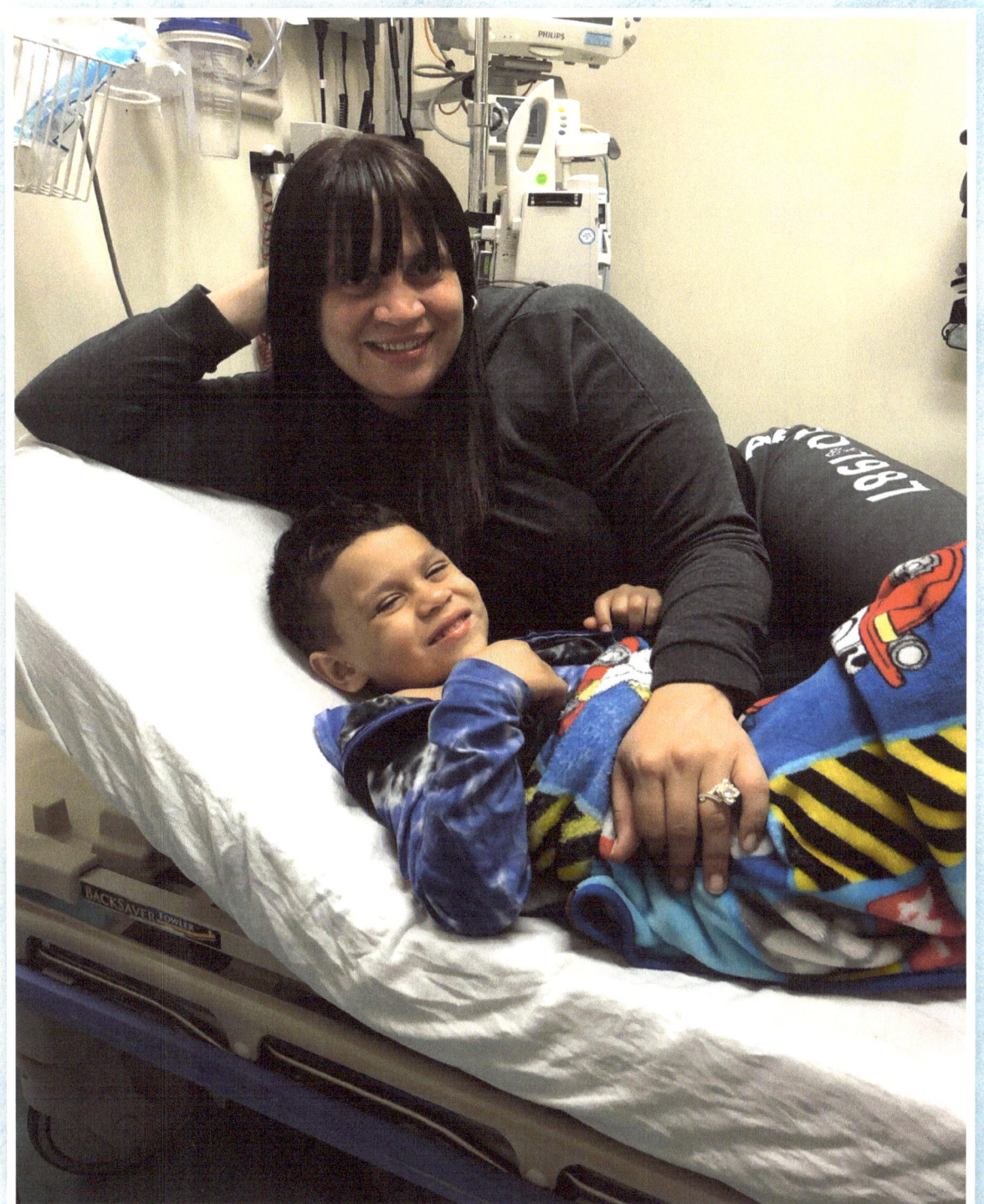

Feeling sick, Isaiah went to the doctor

He was looking for an answer

The doctor's need was much worse than a cold

He muttered, "You have cancer"

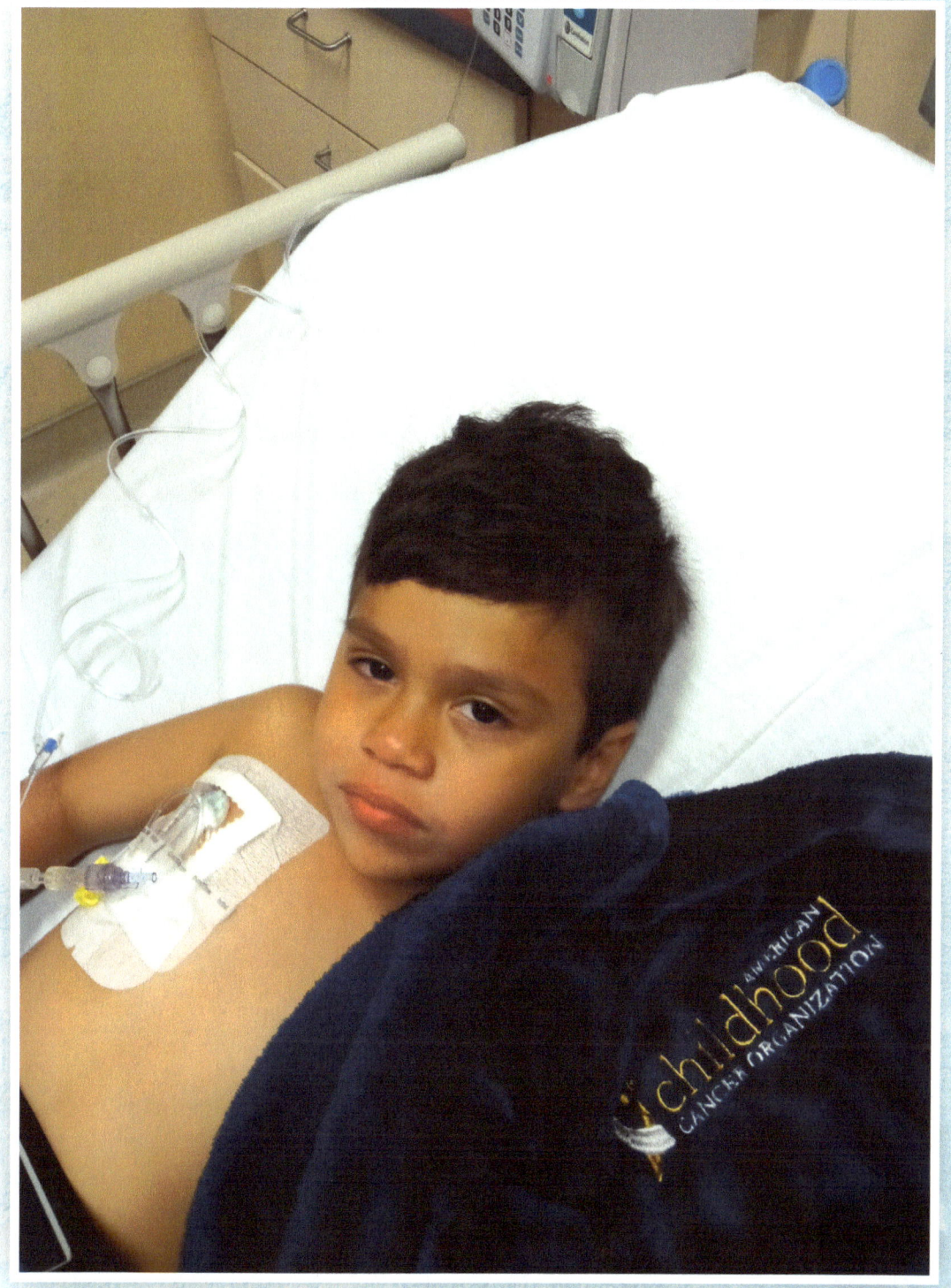

Isaiah and his family could not believe

What they just heard

The doctor's news had

Rocked their world

But Isaiah fought hard

Even though he was rattled

He knew that he was too strong

He would win this battle!

Isaiah fought every day

He is now healed!

He spends his days now

Cruising in his power wheels

Isaiah's future is looking

So much clearer

His illnesses is now just

An object in the rear-view mirror

Now Isaiah is older

He is now grown

The boy who loves superheroes

Is a superhero of his own

We can all learn from Isaiah

Stay positive when things go wrong

Never give up and always fight

Be strong like Isaiah Strong

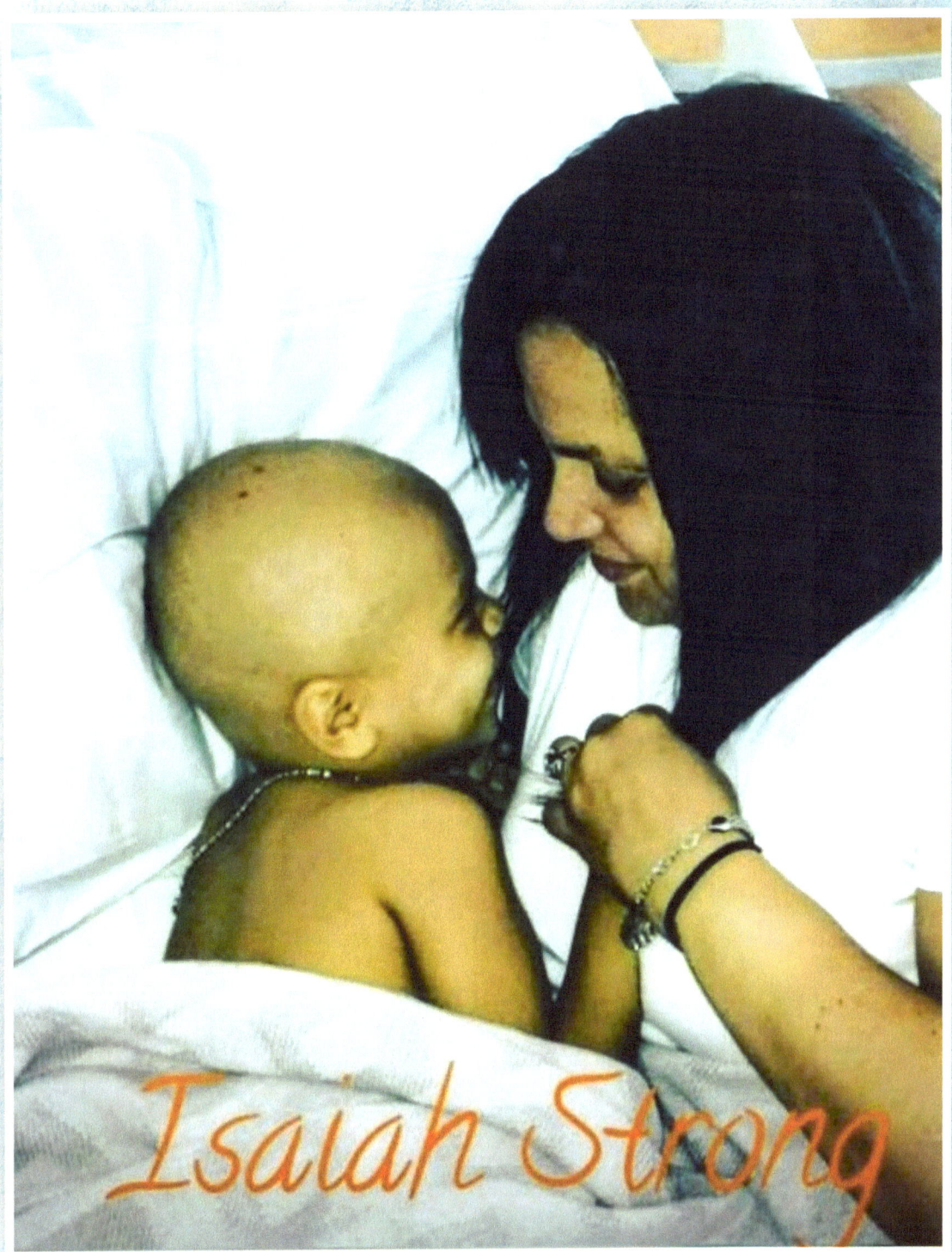

www.ingramcontent.com/pod-product-compliance
Lightning Source LLC
Chambersburg PA
CBHW042027150426
43198CB00002B/93